## *ARRIVAL PRESS*

## *POETIC LIBERTY*

Edited by

TIM SHARP

First published in Great Britain in 1997 by
*ARRIVAL PRESS*
1-2 Wainman Road, Woodston,
Peterborough, PE2 7BU
Telephone (01733) 230762

All Rights Reserved
*Copyright Contributors 1997*
HB ISBN 1 85786 647 9
SB ISBN 1 85786 652 5

# *FOREWORD*

*Poetic Liberty* is an inspirational collection full of moving and dedicated thoughts. As a poet these feelings are both strong and cherished.

These poets write with liberty and strength making this anthology so much more than a collection of feelings, emotion and power leaving you with questions never fully answered.

I hope you enjoy this anthology as much as I did whilst editing it.

Tim Sharp
Editor

# CONTENTS

| | | |
|---|---|---|
| For The Love Of God | Kathleen Fox | 1 |
| Church Wedding | Mary Haslam | 2 |
| Who Am I Kidding? | Grace M Machin | 3 |
| Trouble Where | Elizabeth Docherty | 4 |
| Moving Day | Blanche Bisgrove | 5 |
| Peace And Tranquillity | Paul Clarke | 6 |
| Facing The Weather | Frances Heckler | 7 |
| Christmas Eve In Taunton | David C Southall | 8 |
| What Do I Need? | Joe Caruso | 9 |
| Shelly | Betty Prior | 10 |
| Ye Olde Wishing Well | Danny Kember | 11 |
| From The Heart | Jean Smith | 12 |
| Dartmoor | Mark Taylor | 13 |
| Unfair | Vivienne Doncaster | 14 |
| A Faithful Friend | Elizabeth M Hudson | 15 |
| The Devil's Seed | Christine Armstrong | 16 |
| Trudy 'The Snap' A Lovely Maid | Eileen Holt | 17 |
| Post-Exam Stress | T Hartley | 18 |
| Life | V Weekes | 19 |
| Christmas Lights | V Martyn | 20 |
| Along The Way | Mary Roan | 21 |
| Creation | Natalie Kitson | 22 |
| Dawn | Ruth Smith | 23 |
| The Language Of Flowers | Mary Ward-Hunt | 24 |
| Mangolia Street | Ralf Bates | 25 |
| In Troubled Times | T J Grimwood | 26 |
| You're Meant To Be Here! | Jon Hammond | 27 |
| Love | Ann Rutchak | 29 |
| The Answer Is Always There | Rosie Hues | 30 |
| The Call Of The Sea | Maureen A Jones | 31 |
| Deflowered | Kim Montia | 32 |
| An Easy Catch | M Taylor | 33 |
| Feelings Lost | P Edwards | 34 |
| On A Park Bench | Marie Little | 35 |
| Today's Woman | Joan Jeffries | 36 |

| | | |
|---|---|---|
| Who | Christine Cornes | 37 |
| A Word About Women | Jennie Kitching | 38 |
| For Women Who Feel Scorned | Michaela W Garlick | 39 |
| B Warned | Leslie F Dukes | 40 |
| Gravitations | I Rosie | 41 |
| Nobody's Perfect (A Prayer Away) | Sandra Witt | 42 |
| My Sorrow | James R B McCurdie | 43 |
| Shopping Spree | Sylvia Iveson | 44 |
| Moving Home | Brenda M Hadley | 45 |
| The Fledgling | Mary Joyce Baxter | 46 |
| I Wander Through . . . | Andrea Biggin | 47 |
| Black Is White | Liz Dicken | 48 |
| In Troubled Times | R J Quinlan | 49 |
| In Troubled Times | Pam Chappell | 50 |
| God Loves You | Anne Elizabeth Crockford | 51 |
| All Is Not Lost | Linda Long | 52 |
| The Sign Of The Promise | Nora E Brown | 53 |
| Here's A State Of Things | J Mounter | 54 |
| Eve's Liberation | Dennis Tackley | 55 |
| The Pigeon And The Sparrow | Frederick Hays | 56 |
| Untitled | O Bedford | 58 |
| In Troubled Times | C Cox | 59 |
| Little Mother | Nora M Davidson | 60 |
| Ever With Thee | R J Collins | 61 |
| What A Waste | Daphne Leete | 62 |
| Friends | Lynn | 63 |
| Named By His Father | Alwyn Jolley | 64 |
| R-Day | C M Goode | 65 |
| Me | Enid Gill | 66 |
| Emptiness! | Julie Georgy | 67 |
| Secrets | Ann Swandale | 68 |
| The Gate | K R French | 69 |
| A Moment's Breath | Theo Vasilis | 71 |
| Untitled | Leslie Roberts | 72 |
| A Woeful End | Mary Dickenson | 73 |
| A Memorable Day | H Regan | 76 |
| Where The Wildflower Grows | Christopher James Woodcock | 77 |

| | | |
|---|---|---|
| Heavenly Pursuit | Mary Harris | 79 |
| The Government | Linda Woodhouse | 81 |
| Perfect | A Tolhurst | 82 |
| Every Day's Extinction | Alan Green | 83 |
| 2.50 PM | Arnold Bloomer | 84 |
| Nature Story | Christine Shannon | 85 |
| Everyone Is A Traveller | Kevin J Herbert | 86 |
| Dunblane's Little Angels | Pam Jewell | 87 |
| My Brother | Malcolm Lisle | 88 |
| The Wood | Gordon Burness | 89 |
| Inner Self | Christine Marshall | 90 |
| The Arab | Tara Dougal | 91 |
| Love And Relationships | Ty Allbright | 92 |
| Dawn | Henry Djuritschek | 93 |
| A Soldier's Photograph | Christopher C Jarvis | 94 |
| War-Horse | Francis Parnham | 95 |
| Remembering | Angela A Shaw | 96 |
| Lonely Life | Philip McLynn | 97 |
| Jesus | Louie Horne | 98 |
| I Like To . . . | Steven Richard Lewis | 99 |
| Missing | Dennis Hampton Jeffery | 100 |
| An Irish Guards Soldier | James Hunter | 102 |
| Street Life | John F McCartney | 103 |
| My Friend | Rebecca J Mason | 104 |
| Daddy | C Wyatt | 105 |
| Autumn Winter | Brenda Hinchliffe | 106 |
| Shared Living Shared Loving | Floyd Coggins | 107 |
| Family | Angela Robinson | 108 |
| Food For Thought | Valerie Dunn Karim | 110 |
| Sundays Mostly | John Gordon | 111 |
| Christmas Alone | Isobel Buchanan | 112 |
| My Dear Father | Yvonne Fraser | 114 |
| Where | Florence Brice | 116 |
| Transfixed | Chris Roy Smith | 117 |
| The Echoes At St Francis Of Assisi | Jack Finch | 118 |
| A New Ulster | David Martin | 119 |
| Through The Eyes Of A Child | C M Bellamy | 120 |

| | | |
|---|---|---|
| Forget Me Not | Melvyn Roiter | 121 |
| Blue Sorrow | Priscilla Russell | 122 |
| Society | Chris Batley | 123 |
| Island Of Wealth | David Seymour | 124 |
| Can't Believe | Tom Bull | 125 |
| Race That's Mine | William Flood | 126 |
| Thank You God | Marie Barker | 127 |
| Kick And Rip | Linda Roberts | 128 |

## FOR THE LOVE OF GOD

Our gracious Lord
And King of Kings
Let my thoughts
On silvery wings
Send to Thee in Heaven above
All my prayers and all my love
For in Thee I put my trust
Thou art Lord and Thou art just
When hope is gone and leaves despair
I know O Lord that Thou art there
And so forever I will raise
My thoughts to Thee in heavenly praise
I'll love Thee Lord forever more
Until I reach Thy heavenly shore.

*Kathleen Fox*

## CHURCH WEDDING

Arrangement of flowers in the church today,
The bride will see as she wends her way,
Towards the altar and waiting groom Jay,
He'll hold her hand, the vicar will bless,
Ring on finger for future happiness.

Retire to the vestry for a while,
Then with family for company
Walk back down the aisle.
The bride beams, guests look and smile,
Photos then taken of bride and groom,
Looking forward to their honeymoon.

*Mary Haslam*

## WHO AM I KIDDING?

As I walk in the sunshine, how lucky I am
I can walk freely whenever I can
No fear of snipers with a loaded gun
But I listen to the news about what goes on
I can go to the cinema or drive my car
Look at the moon even count every star
I can sit on a bench in my local park
Sit in my garden hear the dogs bark
Although murders take place, shootings too
No need to rummage for food or stand in a queue
No petrol bombs thrown my way
But I daren't let my children out to play
Don't open your doors two con men on the loose
I wouldn't let 'em in I'm no goose
Is that the sunset I can see, no
Joyriders firing a car glad it don't belong to me
We think we've got it bad, but just seen on TV
Children lying helpless all skin and bone
Sorry must dash and give my pledge over the phone
Next time 'owt goes wrong for me
I won't even moan.
Who am I kidding?

*Grace M Machin*

## TROUBLE WHERE

When in trouble and you see no end
Look to Jesus He is your friend
To keep His rules which do not bend
He made this world which has to end
God plants love not hate
God who made all mankind
In your heart you will find
He will leave no-one behind
Look to God that's what He said
In your trouble you will find a friend.

***Elizabeth Docherty***

## MOVING DAY

We're moving and nothing goes smoothly,
There are boxes all over the floor,
So many items still to be packed.
And the removal-men wait at the door.

Will we ever get everything sorted
I look at the mess with despair,
It's our lives in those cardboard boxes.
Momentos of the past everywhere.

As I wander from doorway to doorway,
Feeling sad to wish it goodbye
I hear the echo of laughter,
The cross words, the fights and the sighs.

Someone else will take all this over
Soon the house will be living once more.
With the hope that our new house accepts us,
For the last time I close the front door.

***Blanche Bisgrove***

## PEACE AND TRANQUILLITY

One fine morning just for a 'lark',
I walked right through the city park,
Not everyone was yet awake,
As I walked past the lovely lake.

There, in the early morning light,
I saw a really pretty sight,
There were lots of ducks and swans.
Standing and waving their magic wands.

Pigeons were running to and fro,
Seagulls with nowhere else to go.
Rooks and crows joined in the fun,
As magpies greeted the rising sun.

Blackbirds, and starlings looked so good,
As they carried out their search for food,
I was moved by the peace I witnessed there,
In the pure, and early morning air.

I stopped for a little while to ponder,
On all the humans, way out yonder,
How wonderful it would really be,
If mankind could live in harmony.

*Paul Clarke*

## FACING THE WEATHER

I battled down Great Pultney Street
Through wind and rain and sleet.
Then the hail came pounding down,
Dancing round my feet.
I struggled with my brolly,
My hat flew off my head.
Like other stalwart shoppers
I wished I'd stayed in bed.
I didn't smile or stop to chat
But hurried on my way.
Everyone looked cold and wet.
It was a dreadful day.

I sauntered down Great Pultney Street.
The sky was cloudless blue.
Everyone was smiling
And saying 'How are you?'
I stopped to talk to Linda
And had a chat with Kate.
No one had to hurry
For fear they might be late.
We all feel so much better
On days when it is sunny.
If someone bottled sunshine
They'd make a lot of money.

*Frances Heckler*

## CHRISTMAS EVE IN TAUNTON

Christmas Eve in Taunton
sitting in a lay-by killing time.
Carols on the radio
sing for auld lang syne
whilst in the town the inns are full
of boozers getting drunk
and three or four young skinheads
kick the spleen out of a punk.

A policeman's dirty panda car
stops by the taxi rank
and he gets out to check the doors
of the Royal National Bank.
Then as the bells of night ring out
the coming Christmas day,
an old bag woman finds a place
to slowly pass away
from ague and hypothermia
whilst midnight masses sing,
their Volvos ringed around the church
'Oh glory to the King.'

The tills rang well these last few weeks
the pre-tax profits soared,
from plastic trash and perfume sprays
the presents, thank the Lord.
Hutus, Tutsies, Bosnicks, Serbs
still fight their bloody wars
and no one seems to give a damn
for others anymore.
Christmas Eve in Taunton,
the streets festooned with lights
is not, by God, or Jesus,
the happiest Christmas night.

*David C Southall*

## What Do I Need?

Well to start with,
I'll need a couple of tons of clay,
and maybe buy a lorry,
to take my work away.

Then there's a studio,
with views all over town,
well I'm sure to need somewhere big,
when I become renowned.

Now I'm going to buy a kiln,
the biggest that they've got,
one that goes 'ping' like a microwave,
when the food is hot.

Now the tools I'll need to work with,
will be three of every kind,
each with a lifetime's guarantee,
and the most expensive I can find.

Then there's the glazes and the colours,
by which to decorate my clay,
yes, this ashtray's going to make me famous
at the V & A.

*Joe Caruso*

## SHELLY

Always faithful,
Always true,
Licks my tears,
When I am blue.
Plenty of long walks,
Plenty of long talks,
No answering back,
Even when on the wrong track.
Give me a dog any day,
Better than humans in every way,
She is the best friend I have ever had,
To lose her will make me very sad.

***Betty Prior***

### YE OLDE WISHING WELL

'E threw in a penny . . . to wish for a pound,
'E slipped on a shillin' . . . fell in an' drowned.
They fished 'im out . . . an' there in 'is pocket,
A wad o' notes stuffed into 'is wallet,

*Greed destroys people!*

**Danny Kember**

# FROM THE HEART

I don't like You very much God
I never will again
You always promised sunshine
And never mentioned rain
Well You've sent it all to pour on me
Rain that ne'er does cease
Have You lost all Your goodness
'Cos You've taken all my peace
You took my mum, You took my dad
You left me deep in sorrow
You never even came and said
There'll be a bright tomorrow
You never came because You knew
The final blow was aimed
What is the matter with You God
Don't you feel so ashamed
The news came several days ago
The doctor told me - true
But I knew where it came from
It came direct from You
So You're taking my beloved
Have You not finished yet
Have I done something terrible
Something You can't forget
Well, You've had Your revenge God
For I am bruised and battered
And all my love for You God
Is gone, it all is shattered.

*Jean Smith*

# DARTMOOR

Tors and denes,
Cows and sheep,
Running streams,
Tramping feet.
Ponies roam,
Quarried stone,
Ruined barns,
Overgrown.

*Mark Taylor*

## UNFAIR

Whilst at the box I stare
I do think it so unfair
That those who cannot see
Have to pay almost the full
Television licence fee!
What thinking lies behind
Something so unkind?

*Vivienne Doncaster*

## A FAITHFUL FRIEND

We had a little doggie
'Lady Whimsey' was her name
We thought at first 'Sir Peter'
But she wasn't of that strain.
She was racing round the compound
In a jolly sort of way
The first time that we saw her
On that happy day in May.

She snuggled up quite closely
Inside my overcoat
As if to say at last you've come
To take me to your home.
She played about quite happily
And chewed up lots of things
She was the bestest sort of dog
That you have ever seen.

For sixteen years she lived with us
Then came that dreadful day
When she was ill, the vet man came
To see her on her way
Up to that great big kennel,
The kennel in the sky
But still we don't forget her
And we never really try.

***Elizabeth M Hudson***

## THE DEVIL'S SEED

The sickness has risen
From the pit of hell,
In the hearts of men
The devil does dwell,
Molesting the mind
With evil depravity,
Torturing the weak
With inhuman savagery,
Man's desire
Is all that matters,
The stench of the orgy
The earth bleeds in tatters,
Used, abused
Dying in pain,
The innocent victims
Cower in shame,
Bloodlust cravings
The murders greed,
Our faith must exorcize
The devil's seed,
Cast out the evil
In your soul,
With prayer to God
Then you'll be whole.

*Christine Armstrong*

## TRUDY 'THE SNAP' A LOVELY MAID

The bride is happy, the groom bemused,
Mother is wishing she'd changed her shoes.
The 'best man', seems to have other thoughts,
Who's that lady in red, looking distraught?
It's Trudy 'The Snap', with camera steady,
The bridal group are poised, they're ready,
Trudy on one knee, her hat pulled down,
Wait; the bridesmaids, are running around.
The sun is out from behind that cloud,
The parents they are looking proud,
Our photographer, Trudy 'The Snap',
Has abandoned tripod, shoes and hat,
It's 'Smile please,' the film rolls on,
Oh dear, the lens cover is still on.
But undeterred, she'll not give up,
The focus is right, and with one eye shut,
A squeeze and flash, the job is done,
But, where are all her subjects gone.
Trudy, 'The Snap', has had her day,
She never will make photography pay.
It's sad this vocation has passed her by,
But she's not the sort to give up and cry.
Well done that maid, tho' it's not your scene.
You're tops for me, for being so keen.

*Eileen Holt*

## POST-EXAM STRESS

I'm tired
My brain's no longer wired
Blown a fuse
Now confused
Hit the booze
Fell, sustained a bruise
Well now I'll have a rest
Looking out over the sea in the south west!

*T Hartley*

## LIFE

What is life but for living
What is pleasure but for giving
What are gifts but for sharing
What are friends but for caring.
What is life but for learning
What is love but for yearning
What is marriage but a ring
Or is it some of everything?

*V Weekes*

## CHRISTMAS LIGHTS

Oh wouldn't it be wonderful
If all the Christmas lights,
Changed into little angels,
And shone around so bright.

They could go to all the places
Where people are alone,
And scatter warmth and friendship
To brighten up their home.

They could go to all the aged
Who struggle frequently,
And help them in their daily chores
Spend time more pleasantly.

They could go to all the hospitals
And take a little cheer,
A gift of fruit or flowers,
A smile to calm their fear.

If only we could find the time
To be little Christmas lights,
Perhaps somebody's Christmas
Could be happier and bright.

*V Martyn*

## ALONG THE WAY

In a quiet country meadow strolling along
Birds in full chorus compete in song.
All around peaceful and clam,
The owls' soft hoot calls from the barn
Pretty wild flowers show off their charm.

Hiding in grasses tall and green,
Silently watching fish in the stream
Two beautiful herons a joy to be seen.
The fox going home to catch up on his dreams.

Boats sailing along in colours bright
The cock pheasant calling,
Letting the world know he was all right
Rabbits come out to play after sleeping all night

Fields of barley and wheat the colour of gold
Things I'll remember, when the year has grown old.

*Mary Roan*

## CREATION

I remember when the world was young
When new life had just begun
Gentle wind brushed through the trees
Hills and meadows, deep valleys
The seas were restless, fresh and cool
The sun shone like a precious jewel
I made a world and a heaven
One who sinned was always forgiven
The animals in their kingdom roamed
Every person had a home
The fishes swam in clear blue seas
Birds flew above the towering trees
Lumbering elephants, crying whales
Men and women, boys and girls
Swamps and grassland, endless beaches
Tranquil forests tall and green
The sky was blue and fresh and clean
Majestic mountains, sandy deserts
I wished the beauty would last forever.

*Natalie Kitson (11)*

## DAWN

This was the start of a new day
As I went walking on my way.
The cows and horses and the sheep
Were still and quiet, all asleep.
They were waiting for the dawn
That heralded a fresh new morn.
Then came the sunrise, creeping slow
That gave the earth a golden glow.
Walking softly through the trees
The sun was dappled through the leaves,
The shady places nice and cool,
Then there was a tiny pool.
Pine cones lay upon the ground
Then there came a sudden sound,
A squirrel ran swiftly from a tree
Then came the buzzing of a bee.
The birds began to sing and then
The world became alive again.

*Ruth Smith*

## THE LANGUAGE OF FLOWERS

I watched a poppy opening through the sunlit day,
a vivid splash of colour, with others on their way,
and soon the clumps of poppies became a blaze of fiery red,
outshining all the other flowers in the long herbaceous bed.
Then all too soon a peony burst upon the scene,
swearing to the poppies that their colours were obscene!
But next a slender cornflower with its little hat of blue,
stood up to stand between them, and said, 'Oh shameful pair you two!
We are all a thing of beauty, God made us all that way
to cheer the sick and lonely, and make a grand display.'

*Mary Ward-Hunt*

## MANGOLIA STREET

She trudged the road at midnight,
her feet unshod yet sure,
a pile of fish upon her head
the higher the phewier.

The baby knotted round her waist
wailed with pune and main;
she chided it in ancient Greek
and begged it to refrain.

Far yonder yet their marbled home
all canopied in knotted tin
gleams in lion lit moonlight;
with djinn filled thoughts she stumbles in.

A grey-haired boy lies by the fire,
an husband and a father both,
to whom, for several skeletons
once plighted she her troth.

There in the dust the holy gruel
gleams in a dull grey heap
and, turning to the shrunken saint
a Christian grace they keep.

'Oh darling Doctor Livingstone
who strolled upon our lake,
our very best forgiveness
please to give . . . and take.'

*Ralf Bates*

## IN TROUBLED TIMES

Each day we hear of trouble or strife,
How someone has been killed or maimed for life,
Another has been murdered or raped or knifed,
Many left without husband or wife.

In this troubled world in which we live,
Many ready to take, few ready to give,
Some have plenty while others starve,
As the rich for themselves a life of luxury carve.

It's all down to selfish desire and greed,
Some have plenty while others live in need,
Nothing seems ever equally shared,
The lives of the rich and the poor uncompared.

But there is coming a time, when a change we shall know,
We shall leave all our troubles down here below,
Those who have served Him and suffered down here,
The Lord will take Home, and in His love share.

But those who have caused all the trouble and grief,
For them there will be little relief,
For their sin and their greed they will be punished 'tis sure,
Because God has promised to level the score.

So be careful how you live, let Him be your guide,
He will be with you whatever betide,
Just trust Him to help you, and guide you right through,
Till home in the glory, we will have life anew.

*T J Grimwood*

## YOU'RE MEANT TO BE HERE!

Maybe you were conceived
through ritual sex
But be released from your
Forefathers' effects.
You may have been born
as a result of Sin
But be Born-Again and
you will want to grin.

If you feel your life is
exceedingly odd
It's time to give yourself
to Jesus *The* God.
He will take away all your
Doubt and your Fear
But only, dear child, if you'll
let Him draw near.

He'll end the sound of that
Primordial Yell
He's infinite power to
break Death and Hell.
He will take you to be
in Heaven with Him
But only if you'll let Him
deal with your Sin.

You'll have to recognise
that you are so Lost
Then you will be led to
stand before the Cross.
And here you will be shown
just how to Repent,
To receive Forgiveness and
be Heaven-sent.

You'll then serve God with
Jesus Christ as your Lord,
Eating and drinking daily
from His pure Word.
You'll want to learn how to
be Honest and Good,
To meet the needs of The
Poor and share your food.

Your life will change and
you will know how to Pray
And worship Lord Jesus and
long for The Day.
You'll look forward to the
time when there's no pain
As you live in Christ and
In Him you will Reign.

Then no more will you moan,
groan, whimper and cry,
All cares will cease the day
you learn to die.
So think about what He
says and don't delay,
The only time to be Born-
Again is Now . . . *Today!*

**Jon Hammond**

## LOVE

We have to let go.
There's nothing to show
Love is like waves on
the shore.
No ripples for us
anymore.
My feelings I'm trying
to hide.
Love has to flow with
the tide.
It ebbs and we go
our own ways
You're gone and I'm left
in a daze.
Love is rough and smooth
Now there's no one left
to soothe.

***Ann Rutchak***

## The Answer Is Always There

Is there anybody here on earth
Who can answer my tearful plea?
For you see I have no wish to stay.
What on earth is holding me!
This plea I put into a prayer,
I put it then was still
With no answer I was left to trust,
to trust in the good Lord's will.
I had said it many, many a time
in the prayer Lord Jesus taught.
'Tis a prayer I seem to set aside
when life to me seems fraught.
When fraught with many a sorrow,
too many! I plead to go.
Then whisper soft 'Thy will be done'
tho' my confusion is on show.
I should trust the One who fashioned me,
Who holds the reason why I'm here
He also holds my daily plans
which to me are never clear.
I must dry my tears and be quite still
for He is working faithfully.
The answer to my prayer is there,
and shall be revealed to me,
On earth I do my learning -
I shall do it patiently.
Till I perfect trust and obedience
and my place is heavenly . . .
Love

*Rosie Hues*

## THE CALL OF THE SEA

I had not realised just how much I missed you
Until I returned one autumn day,
And gazed from the cliff top at the vision of blue,
Out and beyond the span of the bay.

Along the headland the golden path goes winding
To dip behind gorse, now lost from sight.
Emerging in the distance, steadily climbing,
Gracefully snake-like in low, warm light.

The hills, they have lured me away from your presence
To haunting moor and magical fell.
Each beckoning mountain, all fading your essence
With tempting dale and deep forest dell.

As I stand here and listen their spell is broken.
The rhythm of waves, the seabird's cry,
They reach out to me like the call of the siren.
Welcome is there in the soft wind's sigh.

**Maureen A Jones**

## Deflowered

Gun nestling against her head
Arm twisted up her back
Britannia at the mercy
Of a Loyalist attack

She tries to bluff the nation
That she still retains control
Whilst from her captor's tongue
The loyal Orange orders roll

She hides despair with rhetoric
Placates disquiet crowd
And fearful of assailant's anger
Praises him aloud

Submissive to his every wish
And bowing at his feet
Britannia, now deflowered
Surrenders to this gross deceit.

*Kim Montia*

## AN EASY CATCH

Pussy went a-hunting caught a little mouse
held it by the tail and brought it in the house.
I've seen some cats, I've seen some mice
this one really was unique
it had a little fluffy tail and shoes upon its feet.
Where did you get that mouse?
She tweaked her pretty ears
'It was in the barn' she said
'it's lived there years and years.'

*M Taylor*

## FEELINGS LOST

Some say man has no feelings
At times this is true
Like when you look into a man's face
Wondering what he's about

I suppose this is a world for hard feelings
Where the soft are left to melt like butter in a pan
When the heartless centre of a man grows like flint
Does not ache for anyone's agony
Or hears cries - faint like a mist
And it is only a man with a hard heart that doesn't cry.

*P Edwards*

## ON A PARK BENCH

We sit on the park bench, he and I.
He asking me questions of how and why.
Like were the dinosaurs really gigantic,
are there monster fish in the Atlantic.
Who made the sun yellow, round like a ball,
and why do the trees grow so very tall.
When will I grow big enough to reach.
How much sand do we need to make a beach.
Can you do a handstand, not hurting your head,
did you always send daddy off early to bed.
Was grandad once, a little boy like me,
and what are we going to have for tea.
Why do the swallows fly so high.
Where do we go to when we die.
'Come, come' I say 'It's time to go.
All of the answers I do not know.
My head, it feels quite in a spin,
with all your curious questioning.
I only know it's now half-past three,
and we'll have ice-cream for our tea.'

*Marie Little*

## TODAY'S WOMAN

A woman's work is never done, that is what is said.
Housework and shopping, her family to be fed.
She'll have a go at gardening, decorating as well
keeps to a routine, otherwise it's hell.
But if woman ruled the world, there'd be no more wars
Disagreements, *Yes,* then after a pause
one big happy family everywhere there's joy
Making a brighter future for each girl and boy
She can be something of a nag
Is known at times to even brag
Tells the world how she can cope
After she's been watching *'Soap'*
Then does everything to plan
Of course much better than any man
These things are said, not yet proved.
A woman she is, she'll not be moved.
The day has come and there's no doubt
That man knows now, there's a woman about.

*Joan Jeffries*

## Who

My life takes on so many roles
depending on the day,
one minute I'm financier
to sort which bill to pay
I'm nurse to soothe away the pain
and tend the fevered brow,
and mediator I become
to calm the heated row.
When taps just drip and fuses blow
I don my tradesman's hat
and turn my hand to DIY,
(and vet to dog and cat!).
My driving skills are called upon
whenever there's a need,
and navigator's post I take
when there's a map to read.
Detective work I often do
if there's a sock to seek
and teaching skills I would display
with homework, every week.
My culinary arts are used
as waitress and as cook.
For baby-sitting vacancies, well,
they all know where to look.
I'm painter, gardener, to name a few
of all the things I'll be.
I wonder how I find the time
to ever be just me!

*Christine Cornes*

## A Word About Women

A word about women . . . and
The wooing of men
Quite reversed in the thinking of paper and pen
For it's not of the chase, nor of chaste that they write
But the case of the race
In which the two fight
For many a quarrel and many a tear
Is really what brings the two sexes so near

Alone and apart, learn the yearn of the heart
For the warmth of a hug and the time-honoured tug
Of war
Of the souls, both nervous and bold
And longing to hold, though fearing the cold
Of dismay
If either should venture away
And what of the word, about women you ask . . .
The word is a task
A lesson, a mask
Unveiled and unfurled
A very small word
Hell lifting its curtain, shows heaven for certain
When drawn from above
The two understand: their purpose, their goal
Is love.

*Jennie Kitching*

## FOR WOMEN WHO FEEL SCORNED

I'm not a feminist, I don't hate men,
but I stand up for my rights, now and then.
We go through a lot, us women do,
we put up with other people's problems too.
Women groan 'cos men wear the trousers,
but they have to, their legs are awful compared to ours.
We struggle through life to have a say,
we have the same jobs, but different pay.
An egalitarian society, would be ideal,
but this will never be, I feel.
For some women seem to like their lives,
of being beckon calling wives.
If this statement is not the case,
then get up off your seat and make haste.
Things will not happen on their own,
so don't just sit there and moan and groan.
If you want things to take a hold,
then speak out for once, be brave and bold.
There comes a time for everyone,
to tell what they don't want, 'To be gone'.
I know it's not always as easy as that,
but there's plenty of people, to whom you can chat.
Try not to be left on the shelf,
you've got a mind, so think for yourself.
Acknowledge to yourself, you have the right,
gain some confidence, to stand up and fight.
If you believe you are a strong woman,
then you can believe you're as good as any man.
So don't waste your breath on idle chatter,
voice your opinions, they really do matter.

*Michaela W Garlick*

## BE WARNED

A man he needeth more than just a wife
To share life's burdens, and its pleasures, 'but not his wife'!
He could be short, or he may be tall -
But beware, should he be 'A know it all'.
A friend should be a man, constant and true -
There when you need him, and in him confide,
Trusted completely, and to you he never would lie -
But fickle are they that take over your life.
Keep one eye on him, and 'Lock up you wife'!
For should you not follow the words that I've said,
You'll come home one day, and he'll be in your bed,
Your wife will be with him, instead of you, - Now!
He wasn't your 'friend', and she wasn't true,
Now you're regretting those words that I said,
The day that you came home, and found them -
So close, *in your bed.*

*Leslie F Dukes*

## GRAVITATIONS

Lanky was a proud 'un
Who lived up Beehive Street.
Always adorned with a pom-pom tassel,
Bi-lingual with a mousy squeak.

Spontaneous pantomimes were a 'special'
When warbling a sonnet, drear.
Dislodged the wallies, which landed on the floor.
Eruptions were preceded by an explosive sneeze.

Carefully peering beneath the table
A glass eye joined the pursuit.
Now one eye was crossed in amazement.
Following the flutter of a coiffured wig.

In gathering this dispersible collection
Quickly swinging a leg forthwith.
A screw came undone, a foot flew past.
Quarter of Lanky's anatomy was now adrift.

Looney the partner, came home from abroad
to find this uproarious scene.
Lanky being assembled, ere being sent to the Lab.
As a prospective candidate, for a 'loose-living' advert.

***I Rosie***

## Nobody's Perfect (A Prayer Away)

Living a normal life is not easy these days
The world has changed, has some strange ways
You try to defend your own property
Defend yourself against the villain
But he goes free
Or gets a few hours working in the community
If someone entered my house
Especially without my consent
He sure as hell wouldn't leave unscathed
Or, with any contents
I'm so surprised insurance companies today
Haven't got a criminal insurance plan
To pay if they get harmed in any way
And we get tried for GBH against these men
These intruders just laugh in our face
What! Pay 'them' compensation, an utter
Disgrace
It's time to leave this land behind
And find a better place
That is probably harder than we think
Anyway! We'd likely vanish without trace
And never again see the light of day.
A desert island sounds good to me out of
Harms way
That's my wish and hope next time I pray
But a change for the better
Takes longer than a day.

*Sandra Witt*

## My Sorrow

When I feel sad and feel like going mad
I know I have a friend I can turn to
and He will be by my side thru and thru
When I feel pain and feel like swearing God's name in vain
I know He will be by my side and help ease the pain.
He will hold my hand and show me the right way.
of how I can get through my sorrows and stress of each and every day.
I'm glad I have my Heavenly Father to guide me through the night
and the days when I don't feel too bright.

*James R B McCurdie*

## SHOPPING SPREE

A shopping spree is my big treat
I trip to town on fairy feet
no guilty conscience - not today
I'm off to have my wicked way.

I'll buy that dress I saw last week
though seventy pound's an awful cheek
I can't afford it - but I will,
forget I owe that huge gas bill!

It's a mixture of such pretty blues
but it wouldn't go with black court shoes
I'd need some white ones with high heels,
no - I've got to concentrate on meals.

A handbag would be rather nice
and it wouldn't cost me half the price.
I need a loo roll and some soap,
a dish mop, eggs - I'll never cope.

Around the shops on tired feet
who cares about a silly treat
I've got a basket full of food
It's put me in a lovely mood.

So home again - with gas bill paid
and all my plans are neatly laid
sweetheart my husband  - a little flirt!
I've seen a lovely pleated skirt!

*Sylvia Iveson*

## MOVING HOME

Barry and Kathy sold their house one day
'We will move to Nottingham'
They were heard to say
Property guides arrived in the post
Sorting homes they like the most
They trudged around agents with weary feet
Knowing they had a deadline to meet
Came November 29$^{th}$ it was time to move out
No time for regrets, no time for doubt
Furniture lifted into a great big truck
Off to Nottingham and 'Ay up me duck'
All of it then off-loaded onto a farm
To be kept there safely, free from harm
December 14$^{th}$, time to be moving furniture again
All of this hassle becoming a pain
Off to a bungalow in Basford
Their chosen new home
To settle in Nottingham
No more to roam.

*Brenda M Hadley*

## THE FLEDGLING

Through the late days of autumn's gold,
I watched the fledgling's feathers change
Till one by one, from freckled brown,
As if reborn, from dull drab coat
Emerged the scarlet breast.

Each day the fearless little bird
Came to my window sill.
Taking the food that I had placed.
Sometimes my hand, still close
Unheeded by the bird
inspired my hopes that soon, perhaps,
he might feed from my hand.
But patience must be mine.
One false move, the bird might fly.
And then, might not return.

On day he perched upon the fence,
Waiting to come and feed.
A sudden swoop. A flash of red.
Another robin flew,
Its wings outstretched, displayed.
I felt the fear my robin felt
And stood there silently.
Helpless to intervene
As vanquished by a stronger force,
I watched him fly away.

Daily I watched for his return
Placing the food with care.
The winter passed, the year went by.
And though I waited hopefully.
He never came again.

*Mary Joyce Baxter*

# I WANDER THROUGH...

The Blue Blood building stands erect,
Concluding the end of the mall
My feet tread the paved gold slabs
As the night curtain starts to fall.

The circus I approach with wonder,
Though crowded I stand asunder
Watching users do their dealings
My heart goes out with mixed feelings.

In the city's 'Red Light' side
Like parking meters, ladies -
Waiting to be occupied
Curb crawlers out in their number
Pimps' illicit earnings plunder.

The vagabond strums the strings of an old friend
Playing soft music reluctant to offend
His empty cap beside him lays
As he wanders back to better days.

*Andrea Biggin*

## BLACK IS WHITE

When all the white is painted black
and all the black is white,
Somewhere in-between a special light is there
This light will not burn out,
Hold fast to this, it's brighter than the brightest sky.
For you and me when black is black,
The strength it lacks is surely there,
Be still, do not fret, there is more to this than meets the eye.
God is always there, His light will reach you
I know it will, for I've been there.
Bringing understanding, though we may not be fully aware,
it will not leave, it is there . . .
Only in the depths of despair, this light will show,
We have to fall till we fall no more . . .
Before we know that black is really white.

*Liz Dicken*

## IN TROUBLED TIMES

I don't see the colour of the skin.
I look at the heart and soul within
Are they my sisters and brothers
Are we to love each other.

*R J Quinlan*

## IN TROUBLED TIMES

Today I said a tiny prayer
I looked for him and he was there
As he drove past, he waved to me
And minutes later I did see
A smile that said, my love, it's you
I kissed him then, not one but two

Then he went his way. I went mine
From then on all the day was fine
I had to see my friend today
I felt so troubled yesterday
My friend's had troubles, just like me
And at these times, him, I must see

Because I know he helps me so
When all is wrong, to him I'll go
And hope that he will come along
To sing to me, our favourite song
A song that cheers me, once again
It's a feeling, that I can't explain

For he is such a lovely friend
My thoughts for him, they never end.

*Pam Chappell*

## GOD LOVES YOU

Come to Jesus now,
Old and the young,
Meet at the cross,
Every sinner come.

***Anne Elizabeth Crockford***

## ALL IS NOT LOST

'This is my house,' said the field mouse;
Running through paths, amongst golden shafts
Up and down, in and out - always running about.
There's plenty to eat and lots of friends to meet
Watch out! The enemy's about . . .
Quick! High under the straw and watch out for a paw.
My life may be cut short, if I'm caught.

Round, juicy and red, 'I'm perfect,' the apple said
'This looks nice and ripe,' thought the wasp looking for a bite,
'I must have a taste, it's too good to waste.'
Soon there's a hole in the side. 'I'm spoilt!' the apple cried.
'I'm sorry' said the wasp . . . 'all is not lost
I'll cover it with a leaf, no one will see from underneath.

A potato I found, underneath the ground,
I was being rather nosy, looking for somewhere cosy
Where I could hide, when the potato said 'Come inside.'
So I went in one side and out the other, with no bother
So I tried it again, the potato didn't feel any pain.'
Each time it left a hole, right through the soul;
When harvest time came, who was to blame?
The potato was left to rot, that was his lot.

When God created the human race everything was ace,
But Satan had a say and man went his own way.
He didn't obey God's instruction but brought about death and destruction.
Since the fall, man has made a mess of it all
But God had a plan; He wasn't done with man!
By taking a different tack, He made a way back;
Because He died in our place, we've no judgement to face.
Believe Him now, He will show you how.
Only one life - will soon be past; only what's done for Jesus will last.

**Linda Long**

## THE SIGN OF THE PROMISE

Given a rainbow, we'll find our way,
Look on God's promise within every ray.
Blessed creation, strengthen our love,
Raise up our hearts as we see you above.

Given a rainbow, life starts anew:
Throughout our pain God's love carries us through.
This is His promise here in the sky -
Hope to believers that love cannot die.

Given a rainbow, there's no 'goodbye'.
Love just grows stronger as our lives go by;
There in its colours, loved ones we'll greet,
Facing our Maker, we'll kneel at His feet.

*Nora E Brown*

## HERE'S A STATE OF THINGS

The troubles that beset us
Are many, yes indeed.
Folk seem to worship money
And wallow in their greed.

Divorce is on the increase
And so's illicit sex,
And AIDS, and crimes of violence,
Which anyone would vex;

Abuse of children's common,
And mugging of the old,
Wife-beating, husband-bashing
And stealing to get gold.

I cannot cite everything;
That would take far too long.
But can we see a pointer
To where we went so wrong?

I think we can, for surely
God is the Lord of life,
Yet folk back euthanasia
And abortion is rife.

How can we expect, then,
With God to be reconciled
When folk indulge in killing
And other pastimes wild?

We must return to Jesus,
Who only gives true peace,
For all our crimes, divorces
And other things to cease.
He'll help; His love is boundless,
And He will give us peace.

*J Mounter*

## EVE'S LIBERATION

The fairer sex has suffered much
Since mythic Eve the apple touched
Woman has paid the dearer cost
For paradisal blessings lost
It's so unfair

For Adam bit the apple too
A wrongful act as well he knew
To blame sweet Eve for what ensued
Produced a never-ending feud
And deep despair

The macho male has ruled the roost
Injustice and oppression loosed
Domestic life reduced to strife
Frustrations heaped upon the wife
Much inner wear

In cultures that are Bible-based
The male has with indecent haste
His headship based upon the Word
And rarely has his conscience stirred
To be aware

That Eve is in God's image too
That all are equal through and through
That in the Lord all must be one
That Women's Lib and all it's done
Is God's affair

The fairer sex has chains to lose
Too long has man his strength abused
And used the Word to justify
Injustice - now the scriptures cry
The rift repair!

*Dennis Tackley*

## The Pigeon And The Sparrow

Said the pigeon to the sparrow
I'll join you if I may,
This bough will give us time to rest
Before we're on our way,
I'm big and strong; you're small and frail:
My wings are built for speed,
Yours just to hop from tree to tree,
For distance they impede.
My brothers fly from near and far,
New records for to make,
But woodland creature I'm at heart:
No messages I take.
Your sparrow's life's a simple one;
Well known's your appetite:
So eat your fill; grow big and strong,
Thus lengthening your flight.
So little sparrow stay awhile;
Please stop and be my guest.
There's food aplenty, for to eat,
For you and all the rest:
That great provider in the skies,
His wings encircling all,
Invites us, all, to bring and share
Life's joys . . . without the brawl.

This little tale a moral has;
A word for your and I:
God's world today has much to give
For all beneath the sky;
The harvest's good; earth's garners full:
Enough for others too;
The blacks, the whites. The rich, the poor . . .
To *All*, and not the few.

***Frederick Hays***

# Untitled

I write of a young man whose first and only love
was to compete with top riders, racing was in his blood
To break lap records he'd be risking his all
for his passion for racing with no fear of a fall
No interest in girls, smoking or drink
spare parts and entrance fees his wages he'd sink.

Then came a time, he was always in a hurry
He looked ill was losing weight was very short of money
he then confessed, he was beyond despair
borrowed from loan sharks - for his life they had no care

To purchase a new bike to secure his ambition
the reason for this painful admission
I leave out a chapter too gross to relate
weighed in the balances providence held his fate

My story has a happy end cut free
from evil man
He paid off his trebled loan into
their darkest den

I thank God He held a safety net
beneath my youngest son
though my heart is torn for
other boys who fear the drug and gun.

*O Bedford*

## IN TROUBLED TIMES

Never trouble, trouble, till trouble troubles you
An old saying, but very true
Steering through life on its twisted ways
Trouble can blight your happiest days

A trouble shared, is a trouble halved
Through the post comes a happiness card
Not everyone will want to know
That fate has served a thoughtless blow

Comforts seek in troubled times
How to soothe a distressed mind
Trouble in the sky, cause, the rainbow's glow
Lifts the spirits by this coloured show.

Rain in the heart, and no umbrella
Upsets in threes always together
Look for and find, the blue bird of happiness
This earthly trial, 'life's a test'

Troubles hang around like flies
Cast off the gloom, bring bright blue skies
As the old song goes, 'Pack up you troubles
And hopefully they pop away like bubbles.'

*C Cox*

## Little Mother

Mary,

        pondered all these things in her heart,
        Alone, yet not alone,
        Stable enclosure with child enraptured,
        By Joseph befolded, in tranquil serenity
        Mind enlightened, heart illuminated,
        In love, with love
        Will enkindled,
        Alone, yet not alone,
        Time present
        Transmitting time future,
        Future Gethsemene, pierced and piercing.
        Instrument of maturity, stark abyss,
        Cold darkness, suffering endurance,
        Void numbness, ruthless misconception,
        Radiant power, stinging worldliness
        Biting rancour, measure discipline
        Crude depravity
        Wasting, threadbare life
        Fugitive compassion
        Alone, yet not alone
        In quiet confidence solitary integrity,
        Identification in dual identity,
        Silent articulation, solidarity,
        Dignity, service, suffering
        Joyous acceptance, gay abandonment
        Alone, yet not alone
        In love, with love

Mary,

        pondered all these things
        In her heart.

***Nora M Davidson***

## EVER WITH THEE

Of what to write
an empty page
Penny on my mind
youth, that golden age
At the seat of learning
*Wow!* A bet to wage

Changes at home
changes abroad
Almighty God
came with a sword
In troubled times
there the peace
An open book
the title, The
Golden Fleece

And as I write
words anew
A picture remains
loved ones, ever true
Were it not for Thee
and a mightier book
That ever-refreshed I
with that second look
I took

I couldn't put down
hands that pray
In spite of Thee
spied, on the nature
study table
three pailing nails
and a cut of bark
from a cypress tree.

*R J Collins*

## WHAT A WASTE

It seems that business has gone money-mad.
Although there's not much work to be had.
Judging from business mail pushed through my door.
One would think I had money galore.
I used not to mind when the odd one came.
But now many more businesses are doing the same.
I have double-glazing, the council paid for mine.
The improvement it's made to their property is fine.
Others offer insurance, such a big deal.
I'm on National Health, so theirs does not appeal.
Some suggest I learn book-keeping, why bother me?
For all they know, a book-keeper I might be.
Work is offered for me to do at home.
As if I haven't enough, it makes me foam.
I have even been offered shares in a horse,
That went in the bin as a matter of course.
My bankers, surprisingly, seem just as bad.
They appear to have become insurers, it makes me so mad.
Surely saving my money should be their plan,
Not getting me to spend it as fast as they can.
It is necessary for me to spend money, but not all of it.
I must save money for my bankers and I to make a profit.
When I think of the waste of paper and money,
Making extra journeys for my postman, it is not funny.
As there is no bank to post unwanted mail in,
It means I must put it in my own dustbin.

*Daphne Leete*

## FRIENDS

Wen we are young we have few cares.
We take for granted friends around
As we grow older we treasure them more
For true friends are precious I have found.

I'm grateful for those who really care.
They help so much when I feel sad.
My worries and fears with me they share
Rejoice with me when I am glad.

So, thank you God, for these true friends
To help me till my journey ends.

*Lynn*

## NAMED BY HIS FATHER

David prophesied Jesu's resurrection.
'All of us are witnesses to that' said Peter.
Raised to the heights Christ received the Holy Spirit;
Who was promised and whose outpouring you see
As a prophet David knew the oath God swore him
That one of his descendants would succeed him on the throne.
Christ was the one not abandoned to Hades.
The body which did not see corruption was Christ's own.'

When asked about the resurrection of the dead,
Jesus referred to the book of Moses.
'In the passage about the Bush,' He said,
'God told Moses He was Abraham's, Isaac's and Jacob's God.
He is God, not of the dead, but of the living.'
Later, while teaching in the temple, He said
'How can the scribes say Christ is David's son?
When, moved by the Holy Spirit, David calls him Lord?'

Jesus cured a blind and dumb demoniac.
'Can this be David's Son?' astounded people asked.
'He only casts out devils through Beelzebub,'
the Pharisees said.
'Divided kingdoms fall,' said Christ, taking them to task.
'If Satan casts out Satan, how can his kingdom stand?
If through Beelzebub I cast out devils, through
whom did your experts cast them out?
But if through God's Spirit I cast out devils,
The kingdom of God has overtaken you.'

*Alwyn Jolley*

## R-Day

The day I've longed for
Is here at last
And sure enough
I'm leaving fast
No more to rise at dawn each day
And drive along the main north way
No longer have to do that trip
It really did give me the pip

So to you guys I say farewell
And to the others I say . . . O well!
And though you tried to give me hell
I took it all from you old sons
Some for real and some for fun

They say each dog will have his day
At long last mine's here to stay
From now on I'm having fun
And looking after number one.

*C M Goode*

## ME

I'm short, so they're all looking down upon me
They really think I'm just a child
They talk to each other right over my head
Believe me, it drives me quite wild!

They say 'Look my love, are you just kneeling down'
Or 'Are you in a hole?' with a sneer
The clothes and the shoes they are all miles too big
'Try the children's department my dear'

'Isn't she cute?' I hear said as I go
Don't they know I can hear what they say?
But when it comes to finding a seat
I can wriggle through crowds all the way!

Sweet things are wrapped up in small parcels they say,
So's poison I tell them with glee!
Whatever you think about sizes and shapes
I only just want to be me

There's a nicer side too, such protection we get
We're looked after, cherished, it suits.
I'll let this go on just as long as they know
I'm really as tough as old boots!

*Enid Gill*

## EMPTINESS!

Let the one without sin cast the first stone!
That's what I think as I sit all alone.
He was my baby, I loved him true;
But what could I offer, what could I do?
It's easy to point a finger and say
'It wouldn't be allowed, if I had my way.'
But where was their hand, where was their aid,
What did they do for this poor, young maid?
They looked at me sideways, they looked down their nose,
They recited the values of the church's laws.
Thou shall not kill, Thou shall not kill,
And you are a Catholic, so don't take the Pill!
But where is it now, this loving church?
Where is the forgiveness for which I search?
My baby is gone, sucked away,
For the rest of my life I must pay.
Racked with guilt, racked with sorrow
As I wait for each new tomorrow.
What will I do? There is no hope
Because I am ruled by the words of a Pope!

*Julie Georgy*

## SECRETS

The lupin sentinels,
Of rosy hue,
Stand witness,
To the night's
Secrets,
Which pass,
Unnoticed,
By man,
In his slumber.

***Ann Swandale***

## THE GATE

She was waiting at the gate
Such a long long time ago,
I remember it clearly as we celebrate
On that day, our first ever date.

We were both nervous and shy,
No one had told us what joys were to be had,
We talked, and laughed at the silly things
Grew closer together, and the world just slipped by.

We walked in the moonlight, and in the rain
When we parted each night, it gave us such pain,
The days seemed long before our next date
But I knew she would be waiting at that same gate.

By this time we held hands, and walked side by side
Through the meadows, and fields of rich golden corn.
The moon overhead was our only guide,
As we walked through life's richness, so glad to be born.

We were married that year,
That year so long ago
When times were so hard, but we had no fear
What the future would be, or where we would go.

The years that followed, were filled,
With the joys of the family, all being together,
Until the day came when the young ones moved out
A flat on their own, or living together?

Not what we wanted, but they were happy
A change from the days which have long since gone
We get older at first, before we get old
Not realising there is no time in between.

My hair is now silver, once it was brown,
I am so lucky, there is still some to be seen
The wife's golden tresses are still there
Due only, to that loving care.

I still remember that golden corn
And that first ever wonderful date,
And can see her now, with her golden hair
Waiting patiently, at the old farmyard gate.

*** K R French***

## A Moment's Breath

Here within these carnal walls -
Where the tempter's beckoning hand doth call -
This spirit cries so to be free.
'Carnal cage' - doth speak the sage -
'Can I not fortify thee?'
That soul doth yearn to refrain
From pleasures that could thus obtain
Damnation in a timeless place of death.
Cannot the spirit lead when flesh
Succumbs to desire a perilous aim?
That lasts but a moment's breath
And gains us nought but shame.

***Theo Vasilis***

## UNTITLED

There was an old man
who lived in a box,
There was not enough room
For both him and his socks.
He slept with his ears
Sticking out through the lid
And here are some other
Strange things that he did.
He would fold himself up
To get into bed,
Then fry himself breakfast
On top of his head.
He couldn't stand up
So, he walked on his knees
And to blow all the dust out
He just had to sneeze.
He had a TV set
It was such a small size
He could only look at it
With one of his eyes.
Then somebody told him
People live in a *house,*
So he cleared his things out
And sold the box to a mouse.

*Leslie Roberts*

## A Woeful End

Peter Rabbit's in the habit
(Other rabbits do it too!)
Sneaking into people's gardens . . .
Seeing what there is to chew!

Now it is a might off-putting
Growing greens that then get swiped!
Nurturing a precious lettuce
Which gets eaten overnight!

Farmer Fogget,
Cultivator . . .
Market-gardener . . .
Judging shows!
Takes great pride in his prize carrots,
Neatly planted out in rows.

Everyone says he's a wizard!
Got green fingers with his veg!
But he won't take any chances
Round his carrots
puts a hedge.
Now, there is a certain rabbit,
Who loves carrots more than life!
And the rabbit's name is Peter,
Much-loved pet of Fogget's wife.

Near the hutch where Peter's living
Is located Fogget's hedge.
And this rabbit is an *expert,*
Making holes . . .
through which to wedge!

Soon this bunny's sitting pretty,
Nibbling,
gnawing,
guzzling down
Every single prize exhibit
Of a carrot to be found.
In the morning Farmer Fogget
Goes to view his carrot patch.
Finds his precious stock's depleted!
*All* his carrots have been snatched!

Farmer Fogget can't believe it!
His *prize* carrots
*gone astray?*
He determines that the culprit
Must be found
*and made to pay!*
For a week he keeps watch - sleepless -
Busy plotting sweet revenge,
With a rifle and some bullets,
And a Rottweiler from Penge.

For a week he keeps a vigil,
Guarding garden . . . *guarding dog!*
But the only thing he catches
Is a cold, caught in the fog.

For a week there's utter stalemate
Twixt the farmer and the *bun.*
Peter Rabbit's lying *doggo!*
Fogget's dog lies . . .
in the sun.
Then one night old Fogget hears it,
Coming up from near the ground.
Faintly rustly-scratchy noises,
Chomping - gnawing - nibbling sounds.

Peering hard into the darkness,
He detects two floppy ears.
How he *relishes* the moment,
Now the Day of Judgement's here!

Silently . . .
he stalks the rabbit.
Ever closer . . .
he creeps near.
'Til at last his gun's positioned
Right behind the bunny's ear.

See the wicked grin of Fogget!
See him *raise* the loaded gun!
See his trigger finger moving
As he aims
*to shoot that bun!*
Farmer Fogget pulls the trigger.
Rabbit jumps!
The gun's backfired!
Peter Rabbit's gone and hopped it!
Farmer Fogget has *expired!*

When he's laid to rest, his widow
Lays a wreath of carrot-tops
*'In memoriam'.*
The rabbit
Goes and scoffs the blooming lot!
On the tombstone,
in large letters,
Writ for all the world to see -
*'Rabbit cropped it!*
*Musket stopped it!*
*Fogget's copped it . . .*
*RIP'.*

**Mary Dickenson**

## A Memorable Day

South Africa voted as one today
When black and white voters were on their way
To bring forth a democratic way of life
For all men and women, with no more strife
This is God moving in a mysterious way
Caring for his people with love today.

From prisoner to president
Nelson Mandela must have been heaven-sent
To do God's work among his own kith and kin
So the rival government could not win
In spite of the violence that had gone before
He knew all people would be reunited once more.

There are lots of questions to be answered before
South Africa will accept rich and poor.
This is only a beginning, no-one knows the end
When black and white live together and all people are friends
So from now on we hope and pray
That this will be a memorable day.

*H Regan*

## WHERE THE WILDFLOWER GROWS

There is a wildflower that grows
At spring's first light,
Because of my dream on a winter's night
A small green hill where south winds blow,
On broken white wall,
I can still hear you call
Where the wildflower grows.

There is a path I tread so often
In that dream,
Towards that hill
That as I approach
My senses fill
Of ivory so pure,
That face -
With eyes whose parents
Were velvet and lace.

Where the wildflower
Grows apart,
You are kneeling to touch
The flower's heart,
The image of that kneeling grace
With the most angelic face,
Like the imprint of sanctity
Upon a saint.

Where that flower grows
By gentle grass
And grazing does,
The imprint of memory unburned
Forever more,
In dream or choice,
I always hear your voice.

To come back again
Even when I am old,
I shall return again
Until your warmth
Will ease my pain.

Where the wildflower grows,
With rose petals
On the warm wind blows,
And climb that white wall
To see your face,
Till both our spirits
Meet in last embrace.

*Chrisopher James Woodcock*

## HEAVENLY PURSUIT

Here we go
Off to our wonderland
The travelling is long
Body gets weary
Mind is fuddled
The countryside looms, we are there
Tingling, jangled nerves are soothed
Alive once more

The hills are wonderful
Scenery magnificent
Imagination taking over
Boots, shoes, whatever
The weather will decide
Whether one will climb or roam
The rough road, the winding lanes
That leads one on and on

The people are so warm and friendly
Hospitality abounds
With food aplenty
Energy surging through one's body
Anticipation a-gathering
The epic adventure beckons
Where will it lead to no-one knows
But fulfilment at end of day is assured

The scenic beauty that overcomes one
Rippling water cascading down from mountains
Or lying silently, clear and still in lakes
On dark and rough days, all frothy and white
On clear days, all shimmering and bright
Enhancing the beauty all around
For one and all to enjoy
All ages young and old

This place one wonders
Where does it lie
Amongst the roads and towns
Out of polluted struck towns
To open spaces and fresh air
It is to those who love it
Cannot dwell, but love to visit
*Cumbria* in all its glory.

***Mary Harris***

## THE GOVERNMENT

They promise you jobs with plenty of money,
Now that's something I do find funny.
Tax on this tax on that,
Soon it'll be on the dog and the cat.
The Tories have been in for so long,
And still don't know what's right from wrong.
Let's give the others a chance I say,
Maybe they will up our pay.
Look after the old is what I'd do,
Their luxuries are oh so very few.
They need more help to pay their bill,
Empty cupboards that you could fill.
Education is next on my list,
Much better for all do you get my gist.
The millennium is soon drawing near,
So the government needs a kick up the rear.
I really think mums should rule,
They keep things in order and still keep cool.
Just listen you parties to the people's needs,
Bring in someone strong, one who leads
Who can keep up going along the right path,
And get us out of this aftermath.

*Linda Woodhouse*

## Perfect

So perfect was its shape,
Not a jagged edge to be seen,
From lush green to blazing amber,
More colourful, more beautiful than the purest flower,
So neatly formed, so delicately shaped,
And although nothing broke its fall,
Nothing broke,
And yet it lay there, bright and new amongst the waste of the day,
Lost, discarded,
And I thought to myself,
How it could be that something so perfect could be so close to death,
For in life I held perfection,
And in death there was no room for such luxuries,
And yet there it lay, defying all I knew to be true,
And as I wandered the image of this small, yellow, leaf returned to my mind time and time again,
. . . Too perfect to die today I thought.

*A Tolhurst*

## EVERY DAY'S EXTINCTION

I want to write this poem
To try to make you see
All the problems of the world
To see that they are real
I will tell you of the pollution
That we pour into the seas
No more forest left
We have chopped down all the trees
Elephants are fewer
The whales are even less
Every day's extinction
Until there's nothing left.

*Alan Green*

## 2.50 PM

'Stands the church clock at ten to three?
And is there honey still for tea?'
Perhaps the best known lines of Rupert Brooke -
although 'If I should die . . .' is more sublime.

Now Brooke's dichotomy in looking back
and forth translates in us the same desire
to store some memories and hopes of what
we can transport from life on Earth to keep
alive the lessons learned from being aware.

Some backward glances; when my mother died,
the doctor smiling, but no words exchanged,
as if I didn't realise the moment;
that time I drove too fast, believing
I was in a real Grand Prix, a winner,
outpacing all the champions of the world
(but really only in a country lane);
the moment when Patricia turned me down,
a tear suspended on her freckled cheek.

So, where's the honey in a second life?
No ageing, poverty or grand divorce,
no illness, accident or pain to spoil
existence in unending static bliss?
Is that what Rupert Brooke by 'honey' meant?

*Arnold Bloomer*

## NATURE STORY

*Beauty* shows in a flower,
A rose is like a heart,
Delicate are its petals,
If touched can fall apart.

*Love* resembles an orchid,
Blooming romantic bliss,
Shared with someone special,
It's as gentle as a kiss.

*Hatred* would be a nettle,
Stinging its poison so mean,
Striking when you're not looking,
Leaving its mark to be seen.

*Peace* would be an olive leaf,
Carried by a dove,
Flying through a sunset,
Embracing us with God's love.

**Christine Shannon**

## EVERYONE IS A TRAVELLER

Time: a grain of eternity, not
equal to a raindrop in a vast
ocean.

Eternity awaits the soul,
everyone is being swept along a
road that leads to death.

God has carved out a narrow road
that leads to life.

Everyone is a traveller, time
sets the pace, it never stops, it
drags you along, whatever road
you are on, it can drag you into
hell or lead you into heaven.
No-one can stop it, it ticks away
your life, it is an invisible current,
sweeping you along to your eternal home.

A few have escaped the broad
road, and have taken the narrow way of
the cross, you have to travel light
on this road, no room for baggage,
it is a rich man's nightmare, you can
only squeeze through if you drop it all.

*Kevin J Herbert*

## DUNBLANE'S LITTLE ANGELS

Dear God you have the Dunblane children
Up in heaven by your side
Getting all the love, that you so freely give
On the 13$^{th}$ March 1996
The children entered school, like any other day
As they were having fun
With their teacher in the gym
A man walked through the door
In his hand he held a gun
He pointed it and then he fired
Young children lay injured and dying on the floor
The teacher also died, people were very shocked indeed
It was very difficult to accept
That so many little lives
Had been taken in such a way
Many a tear was shed that day
Feelings of sympathy went out to the parents
And to everyone involved
Life goes on as usual, for all those left behind
A lot of pain they have to daily bear
But comfort is gathered from knowing
Their friends are always there
When they are feeling down and need to cry
Or want to talk about their loss
Dunblane's little angels were very greatly loved
And happy memories they have left behind
They are up in heaven with their friends.
They will never be alone
No more pain will they ever feel again
Happy they will always be.    Amen

*Pam Jewell*

## My Brother

Who gets drunk at 3am,
Comes round to my house again
Cut and bruised from fighting men?
My brother.

I tell him he should go away,
Tomorrow is a working day,
I need some sleep to earn my pay.

'Sorry to hear that but I need to borrow some money.'
His doctor says it does no good,
The clinic at Collingwood,
It's too close to the village pub.

We even tried the AA too,
My brother was sick in the loo
And they didn't know what to do.

Help me, help me, someone please,
My brother has a strange disease
That nothing in the world can ease.

*Malcolm Lisle*

## THE WOOD

I know a wood where no-one goes:
Where no paths lead, which no chart shows.
Where summer sighs and winter blows,
And no man sees or hears or knows.

There, no axe falls, nor other dread
Ambition with its heavy tread
And noisome clamour of the dead,
Disrupts the sylvan harmony.

But once, on a halcyon summer's day,
Just once, I trespassed, fearfully.
And there, in a grassy dell she lay,
Her golden hair adrift, astray,
Amidst the trembling harebells.

Her eyes, the blue of summer skies;
Her mouth, a petalled, pink divide,
Desire smiled from her elfin form:
We touched; the shadowed glade grew warm.
Her satin skin, her breath sublime,
Of honeysuckle, sage and thyme,
Enveloped me upon the hour
As lifetimes passed in that verdant bower.

We laughed and loved, then slept anon,
I woke, reached out, but the maid had gone,
And herbs and grasses where she'd lain,
Stood straight, unpressed against my hand,
As if she'd never been.

I know a wood which once knew me,
Now, under its latticed canopy,
Where winter's midnight wind blows free,
I wait, content, as she sings to me.

*Gordon Burness*

## INNER SELF

A hurtful word cuts like a knife
crushing you in an instant and
can take years to heal the memory.
Just as a word of encouragement
can lift your spirits, causing you
to hold your head high.
What a responsibility we have in our interactions
with each other! That knowingly, we can build
or destroy one's self-esteem, which sets
us on the road of life, forming characters
of the person we are yet to become.

*Christine Marshall*

## THE ARAB

Sleek and slender
her body divine
with natural beauty
I wish she was mine

Her Arab tail pointed
up towards the sky.
Her nostrils were flaring
there was fire in her eye

Her ears were pricked forward
she was as grey as the moon
then she disappeared into the darkness
to reappear soon.

*Tara Dougal (11)*

## LOVE AND RELATIONSHIPS

When two hearts pull together, love is so alive
like a flower nurtured by sun and rain, to survive
the seeds from this flower, will find the rain and sun
born of two hearts, that became one.

*Ty Allbright*

## Dawn

No lovelier could there be
for when the sky meets the sun
No lovelier could there be
than dawn for all the world to see.
For words were never made
that could describe the beauty
that my eyes see
For you are sunrise
that awakens my heart
and you are dawn
that starts a perfect day.

*Henry Djuritschek*

# A Soldier's Photograph

I found it on a market stall, a husband now I guess,
With a new wife, for a new life, hoping to progress.
They are in their wedding finery, she in billowing floral bonnet,
He with soldier's uniform, starched collar, chin propped and
resting proud upon it.
But now sepia shadows only recreate his existence,
As a century ago he looked into the eyes of a studio photographer,
Now across that gulf of years, and tears,
He now looks into mine.

How fragile, impermanent, how brief our own existence seems,
When time can turn us all to dust like photographs' lost sheens.
This curse of the camera, one click and we are caught, frozen forever,
Ageless with eternal youth, by proxy and without thought.

His life was full of mystery, adventure good and lust,
But time had swallowed him, one shot, returning him back to dust.
The photograph was there, square, black, white without its
modern sheen,
Telling him, you have been seen.
Then, a melancholy of thought occurred,
The photograph, faded and forlorn,
Will a stranger, in a century of time, pick up the photograph
And wonder whose lives were torn?

*Christopher C Jarvis*

## WAR-HORSE

A mighty beast dappled grey, a war-horse falls along the way
Cannon-fire, musket balls, reach their target, the war-horse falls.
A bloody beast, ravaged by man.
Abused by armies since time began.

Blood on hoof, then gallop's stopped
One beast less, when the war-horse drops.
The horse has no concept of fighting a war
Cannot understand what the killing is for.

A magnificent beast, a trusty steed,
Is left on the ground by mankind to bleed.

*Francis Parnham*

## REMEMBERING

If you go to Holland to remember the war,
Some people won't accept it and say it's a bore.
There's a Holocaust Memorial with very sacred grass,
Lots of other horrific memories of days that are past.
Three stones of different colours representing dead children, women and men,
The monstrosities are unbelievable and must never happen again.
In Amsterdam there's Anne Frank's hiding place,
What her family went through because of their race,
Our young English soldiers fought and died,
They went bravely into battle, no feelings could they hide.

What a disastrous loss of life,
Not to ever see their mother or wife.
What does it prove, what do you gain?
To start a war, you must be insane.

*Angela A Shaw*

## LONELY LIFE

She goes to the coastline
And looks out to sea
Says 'When is my sailor boy
Coming for me?'

She goes down at midnight
And comes back at dawn
But no-one will tell her
Her search is forlorn.

She goes to the seashore
Her eyes scan the coast
But no-one will tell her
Her man is a ghost.

The sailors were heroes
The soldiers were brave
But they lie side by side
In their cold lonely graves.

*Philip McLynn*

## JESUS

Jesus - my point of reference is He
As to what God is, and what man is to be.

*Louie Horne*

## I Like To...

I like to paint
I like to walk
I like to climb
I like to talk.

I like science
History too
I like nature
At the zoo.

I really like all the above
But one thing I'd really love
Is to sell my paintings
And buy a mansion,
And a Ferrari to park outside
on the drive.

*Steven Richard Lewis (9)*

## MISSING

They were my crew,
but now they're gone
Bill, Jock, Dai
And Pilot, Ron.

'Skip' came to me
and smiled and said
I've a request
from your pal, Ted.

He needs another flight
just one raid more
He'll be off 'ops' then
finished his tour.

He has a wife and kid
she worries a lot
Only one more trip
that's all he's got.

I had always thought
we would all go together
Crash on take-off
flak or foul weather.

But I agreed
he could fly in my stead
He would be in my turret
I would be in my bed.

I joined them in the Crew Room
Thermos, map and scarves
Usual well-worn jokes
loud nervous laughs.

We all waved from the Tower
the target was Cologne,
Now the telegrams are sent
*Missing',* and I am alone.

***Dennis Hampton Jeffery***

## AN IRISH GUARDS SOLDIER

His name was William Johnstone a small pork van he drove
To go about the country lanes and keep his customers happy
For this very pleasant Willie's aim in life was to help all folk alive,
His other love in life was the music of the Pipes

What an impressive lad he looked with his kilt of Royal Stewart
and busby tall and his belt and buckles shining bright,
to keep the pipers on the beat was his great ambition,
and when to a contest they did go they were sure to win the Cup.

But then the war alas did come and he did join the Colours
and to the Irish Guards was accepted and they were sure
impressed only now he wore the Red and Blue to carry the
big bass drum to keep the regiment in step.

But then so sad to Italy the regiment it was sent to clear
the Anzio beachhead and chase the Nazis home.

His comrades he did well attend for a stretcher bearer he was
But fate it took an evil hand to end his days of music
For down there came a German shell and ended Willie's life.
So all you Irish Guardsmen when you march to the pipes and drums
Look up, look tall and be very proud of the drummer
who gave it his all.
*And the band played the 'Flowers of the Forest'.*

*James Hunter*

## STREET LIFE

Silence scuffles betray
The human sanctuaries
Of ragged boxes;
Spreadsheet newsprint insulates
The cold, the world
And hides the restless sleeper.

Alone in his domain
Companion to a fitful cough
Night dew wets his foggy breath;
While pavement cold seeps through
The paper layers
To numb his toes.

His the lumpy custard life
Flailing silent in the deepest end
All dignity excised by fate;
Respect the least of virtues
As dawn scythes the icy sky
Heralded by dust-lorry click and hiss.

*John F McCartney*

## MY FRIEND

Laugh my friend
forget the times
that make you sad
and bring you down
I'll be there
your faithful clown
to make you glad
I'll always say
'I'm here.'

*Rebecca J Mason*

## Daddy

Hello, Lord! How are you?
Good, I hope.
Er, right. Yes. Just to say thanks really.
You know, for food and all that.
Oh - could you look after those
Little poor kids on the News?
Cheers. Great.
Well, just about wraps it up really.
So . . . Amen!

Daddy? Wait. I
Wanted to tell you, before I go to sleep,
I wanted to say
I can't do it without you.
I'm not strong enough on my own.
You're the best, the absolute best,
And I love you more than anyone
And I'm sorry when I screw up
Please don't give up on me
Please don't let go
Forgive me.
And sometimes that's what gets me through the day.
Unconditional love. Thank goodness!
Thank you.
So, tomorrow . . . Let's do it together, yeah?
Only this time, can you lead the way?

*C Wyatt*

## AUTUMN WINDS

The sky is not for you or I, it's Mother Nature saying goodbye,
To the sky saying spring and summer is goodbye for you and I,
for another time.
Flowers will die but, another season from the autumn winds will
re-season to the next blue sky.

Spring will tell us there is another blue sky, daffodils will
bloom and tulips will glow, to spring to Mother Nature as
will show, flowers and roses will always grow for us to know.

Autumn winds, springtime, summer and again to autumn winds
but, Mother Nature will always win, unless we destroy the
environment within.

Spring, summer and autumn winds cause leaves to fall and
replenish therein.

*Brenda Hinchliffe*

## SHARED LIVING SHARED LOVING

Of all the things that we vowed to share
The difference in our age is neither
here nor there
For I am twenty-two and you are twenty-one
The six months that separates us has been
there since time begun

But once a year on this fair day
Love does find its own sweet way
To show to you what's good and true
For today my love you're also twenty-two

But soon the page of life shall turn
And for this day again I'll yearn
But with you near the pain I will bear
Until again our age we share.

*Floyd Coggins*

# FAMILY

We were a family like many another,
Mother, father, sister and brother and another
and another and another!
First there was me
and when I was three,
I had to share my mother
With David my brother.

It was hard for me to understand.
A sister Patricia had been planned.
I had been told she would come to play,
I did not expect a two-year delay!

When they came they were too small,
I could not play with them at all!
When I was seven Susan was born,
Small and weak, a child forlorn.

I thought it was all over then
but Elisabeth came when I was nearly ten!
The party should have been for me,
But the baby was all they wanted to see!

Sometimes I thought it was heaven
When we went out together, yes, all seven.
We hadn't a car in those far-off days
So we all rode bicycles along country ways.

Time passed by with laughter and tears.
Then each one left to follow careers.
This meant that times together were few
But the bonds between us steadily grew.

Now we are just sisters four
Mother, father, brother no more,
We live far apart but support each other,
We are a family like many another.

*Angela Robinson*

## FOOD FOR THOUGHT

Pensioners were your parents,
But now you've reached this stage,
Life is not as we expected
As we ourselves have aged,
People will go without essentials,
Just to save a bob or two,
Now it will be your turn soon,
So what are you going to do?

I want to see our pensioners with a greater say,
Ensuring that their voice is heard
each and every day,
Falling standards need restoring,
To keep the status quo,
So use your influence while you can
Because you have not far to go!
Perhaps your partner has passed on
before your span's complete,
But realise you are not alone isolated in defeat,
We have to go to war all over again!
Use your mouths and join in,
Even if house-bound, don't forget to use your pen.
The pen is mightier than the sword,
So the proverb goes,
So don't let them get away with their apathy,
In this nuclear society,
Let's rejoice the golden years in health,
wealth and security,

That's the way it should be!

*Valerie Dunn Karim*

## SUNDAYS MOSTLY

the faded memorial stones
to persons now unknown
have seen many congregations
going through the motions
sundays mostly
cold air, white hair, ghostly

large bible read on
golden eagle lectern;
here endeth the first lesson
and, later, here endeth the second

prayers for the royal family and the dying
prayers for big business and the lying
mumbled prayers by rote emerge,
hymns flattened to a tuneless dirge

well-to-do pillars of the community,
sober-suited, big-hatted, overdressed,
keeping up appearances, maybe,
and the lonely and the dispossessed
and a few from the evangelical tendency

inattentive children ask can we go now,
mum it's cold, what's for dinner?
in his sermon reverend howe
regrets the organist mrs winner
has run off with deacon hughes
creaky half-empty pews,
yawns barely stifled,
leaky roof, restoration fund news
tea in the church hall after, and trifles

i see the breath before my face
why do i come? maybe god's on my case

*John Gordon*

## CHRISTMAS ALONE

Now it's the time of year,
For bells to ring, a coming new year,
Shops so busy, people rush by,
They don't have time to sigh,

They throw some money in a tin,
But not enough to buy a din,
It's Christmas, I have no money,
But I've got the will to tell somebody,

The snow lies deep, my shoes, they leak,
My body's cold I hardly sleep,
In shop doorways in a sleeping bag,
I roll a cig then have a drag,

People pass they only stare,
An' leave some money, they can spare,
Christmas time I dream of home,
And wonder, why am I alone?

Today is Christmas, I'm out in the street,
A policeman calls asks me to move on,
I ask him what did I do wrong,
Then swore at him and don't know why,
He locked me in a cell warm and dry,
Now I'm home I sit an' cry.

A turkey dinner I roll a cig, then have a drag,
The police give me a sleeping bag.
The snow falls it lies so deep,
My shop doorway, all covered in sleet.

A kind man gave me a scarf, some socks,
Now, I'm happy, I've got a box,
I walk along in the snow,
Wondering, just where to go,

A summer seat, no-one there,
I sit a while, an' say a prayèr,
Then lie down to sleep once more,
When I awake, nice and warm,
With all my family who were gone,
All together we will be,
*Up in heaven, a family tree!*

**Isobel Buchanan**

## MY DEAR FATHER
*(Dedicated to my dear father, love you always.)*

I still know dear Father,
That you love me and me you adore.
You worry needlessly and continuously,
Till at last you hear me,
Enter through the front door.
Our special bond,
Our friendship, will flourish in my life.
I still see that day, your silent fallen tear,
The day I married and became, my husband's wife.
You thought you had lost me, your daughter,
Yet deep down you had gained,
A good son-in-law, you really found.
Alas! A paralysing stroke you had,
Sadly to make you wheelchair bound.
Crabby, bitter you appear to be,
Only, I can understand, I know how you really feel.
It's very cruel a stroke,
Your independence and dignity it can steal.
Even though times seem hard, frustrating.
I still love you, very much too.
It's my turn, to reverse the role and look after you.
It's my turn now, to worry and fret and show I care,
In a different way, to understand your distant stare.
I can tell by your face you need,
Cheering up, a good laugh and a shared joke.
Stimulation, a different interest, teasingly I poke.
I hope I am the daughter you wanted me to be.
Always there, that special bond, between you and me.
I know my visits are special to you,
You relax and seem far more happy,
Remain dear Father, my good friend, cherished by me
At the window steady you sit, watching, waiting,
Passing a long day, till you see me returning.
The paper you read from cover to cover, well read,
Or your ear to the scanner,

A voice distant, a pilot in a jet, to be heard.
My dear Father, a distinguished person,
A diplomatic good friend.
I still see the humorous person,
More interested, reliable, on whom I can depend.
A special person, a bond between Father and daughter shared.
Throughout our duration, he's shown he really cared.

***Yvonne Fraser***

## WHERE

They say he picked me up, and carried me.
I felt nought.
They say he was there, when I called.
I heard nought.
They say when I felt low and down
He said nought.
And yet what was there?
Was it nought?
I didn't see. I didn't hear. I didn't feel.
Yet something or someone was.
But who was there . . . ?
It must have been *'Him'*.
Because now I can feel. Now I can call and now I can see.
*It must be He!*

***Florence Brice***

## TRANSFIXED

Fixed, the needles score the wrists -
Metal blow on metal blow
Bites the wood and hammers up the pain.
Turn your face, this pain stains the tree
And will not drain away the agony of grief.
Rough wood racks your back and shoots up veins
Itching the sweat into streams of screams.
Hate jolts upright an innocent man,
Yet the eyes, glazed, still shine love.
Barabbas this was your post; breathe deep.

Thorns sink scalpwards,
Blood paints runnels over bony shoulders,
Exhaustion suffocates the mind and bleeds homewards.
A pain-drenched forehead splits at brow and tears
into the Temple.
A sign spikes the crime *'King of the Jews'*.
History hangs in balance;
Time heals nothing -
These unjust wounds bleed forever.
Aching limbs push up blisters, my sin inflames the joints;
God, in control, leaves His Son to rot on a cross for me.

***ChrisRoy Smith***

# THE ECHOES OF ST FRANCIS AT ASSISI

Very little has been changed by eight hundred years
For the small hillside town of Assisi.
Nothing at all has been changed by eight hundred years
In the message Saint Francis gave the world,

It was there that his first followers worked with him,
Living in rough shelters they built nearby,
By the chapel, the Portiuncula so dear
To his heart, and to the rest of his life.

After a few more years the Order had grown great,
In its numbers, and five thousand brothers
From Italy, France, and Spain, gathered together
In a space by the Portiuncula.

Lying in the Basilica of Saint Francis
Is the tomb of the well-loved holy man.
Four followers are buried near - they are Leo,
Rufino, Angelo and Masseo.

Perhaps the humblest of men, if he were alive,
Would be shocked at the sheer size and grandeur
Of the great Basilica, where his pilgrims flock,
Graced by great frescoes, some by Giotto.

Lying down in the valley, below Assisi,
Is yet another great Basilica,
Saint Mary of the Angels, and, inside its walls,
Still stands the tiny Portiuncula.

In this same modest chapel Francis asked to die,
Ending his ministry where he started
To send his message of love - and serving the poor -
To the whole world, and to the end of time.

*Jack Finch*

## A New Ulster

Rifled and reduced to rubble
Our land can still rise
Above the paramilitaries
To God's paradise.
We are standing at the cross-roads,
The cross is the key
That can open Heaven's window
To rain liberty.
The tombstone of human wisdom,
Of our ability,
Or political manoeuvres,
Shall be rolled away.

*David Martin*

## THROUGH THE EYES OF A CHILD

A small girl, clutching tightly to her Mother's hand,
Her first day at school, little heart pounding, tears very close.
A small boy, holding back at those big school gates,
His first day at school, new shoes pinching, trying to be brave.

The school day now over, two small children hand in hand
Come into the sunlight, their eyes full of wonder, tears now gone.
Anxious mothers reclaim their children and journey home.
The small girl waves and the small boy waves back.

The Mother asks 'What is that little boy's name?'
'Which little boy?' The small girl enquires.
'Your new little friend, the little black boy.'
The child looks up, puzzled, 'Which little black boy?'
'The little black boy, who was holding your hand.'

'Oh! That was Andrew,' the child replied
'Is he black? Oh, I didn't know that.
He draws the best pictures in all of our class
And he's going to be my best friend.'

*C M Bellamy*

## FORGET ME NOT
*(Dedicated to Nellie, my mother-in-law)*

I'm getting old
Forget me not
I knew Hyde Park
When a flower-pot
In Trinity church
I met my doom
Now we live
In an old back room
When you're down
Just look up
Uppity up
Uppity up
Remember me
Forget the rot
Forget me not
Forget me not.

*Melvyn Roiter*

## BLUE SORROW
*(To a man I admire)*

Yesterday was an inspiration to me
as only people who actually see.
I met a blind man by the seashore
and it was not me he was looking for.
I asked him what he was doing and he simply replied.
'I am looking for my eyes.'
I quizzically looked at him and asked if
he had ever seen the colour blue.
He laughed and answered 'Dreams do come true.'
He put out his hand and showed an ink stain
'Yes I can smell it.'
I asked if he could feel the colour
the answer was simple and with sorrow
'That is why I come to the sea.'
He laughed 'It is the riverside and it is not blue!'
He gave me a wink!
He truly knew the colour blue and
didn't need sympathy from me or you.

*Priscilla Russell*

## SOCIETY

*Lord,* Your heart must bleed when you see
young kids strutting around our streets
or sitting about in a dazed state
hitting out in violence to get their kicks.
Where are the authorities
when the pushers are around
selling their wares to a twelve-year-old?
Someone's daughter or a friend
sells their body as a means to an end.
Why doesn't someone intervene?
It's not just in our cities,
it's in high society everywhere
only You can stem the tide
to stop the rot sweeping through our land.
Lord, Your heart is bleeding for You see
man's greed and depravity.

*Chris Batley*

## ISLAND OF WEALTH

Island of wealth in seas of destitution,
This septic isle, this institution,
Is washed by oceans full of tears,
And nobody sees, and nobody hears.

Harbouring riches against the rising seas
Of dissidents and refugees
Who swim across the narrow straits,
And nobody stops, and nobody waits.

We build our walls of stone to keep away
The rolling waves, to keep at bay
The ones who plead, the hands that reach,
But still they wash up on the beach.
We make bastions of our greed,
Battlements against their need.

*David Seymour*

## CAN'T BELIEVE

Having a belief in God is something
I find impossible to do.
But how I envy those who
are able to.

What comfort they must get in
times of need, when they call
on God for help, knowing
he'll take heed.

Knowing he'll listen to all their
sorrows and joys, like a
loyal friend, and be by their
side to the very end.

I'll never have this comfort of
God's presence, and for that I
know I'll be that much poor.
But I'll never be able to
believe in him, of that I'm sure.

*Tom Bull*

## RACE THAT'S MINE

I met a race of people tonight
that's different to my own.
They wined and dined and pleased me
yet they treat my like with scorn,
I was brought up to be wary
never to get too close,
our geography divides us,
our history's a joke,
is my God an ugly reason
to be hated and abused,
Or is God the only reason
that makes us all confused!

Who cares what you think
or what you feel within,
who cares about religion
or the colour of your skin,
have I got tunnel vision
or am I allergic to the truth,
what has history taught me
in my unsuspecting youth,
I'm in my early thirties now
still playing their silly games,
it's only now I realise
in the end, we're all the same.

*William Flood*

## THANK YOU GOD

Thank you God
For Mum and Dad
For two more Sisters
and life in the country!

For Food and Drink
and a wash at the Sink
For a roasting good fire
and suitable attire!

For lots or mirth
and love of the earth!
For agility and spring
and happiness to sing!

For Church and home
A place to be grown
For friends and pals
Be they fellas or gals!

*Marie Barker*

## KICK AND RIP

Dancing away at the local disco
For a laugh I did a high kick
My friend Jill said she'd have a go
In her tight skirt - with a split!
      As she tried the kick
There was a loud rip -
Her skirt had ripped right up the back
I started laughing and giggling
She said 'Run and get my Mac'
I couldn't move my sides were splitting -
Her face went bright red.
Like the G-string she had on
'Help me' she said
As everyone was staring at her bottom -
Her hands went over her face
But that wasn't what she had to hide!
That was the wrong place -
It should have been her backside.
      We disappeared quick
      Out of the fire exit -
I was still giggling as she looked at me
She started to smile - then it turned into a laugh
Which she couldn't do before - now it was funny
As she looked at her skirt ripped nearly in half.

*Linda Roberts*

# INFORMATION

We hope you have enjoyed reading this book - and that you will continue to enjoy it in the coming years.

If you like reading and writing poetry drop us a line, or give us a call, and we'll send you a free information pack.

Write to :-

**Arrival Press Information**
**1-2 Wainman Road**
**Woodston**
**Peterborough**
**PE2 7BU**
**(01733) 230762**